O

Care is a Four-Letter Verb

Care is a Four-Letter Verb

By Molly O'Dell

WordTech Editions

spring poems
molly -
2006 - 2010 in Nebraska

Published by WordTech Editions
P.O. Box 541106
Cincinnati, OH 45254-1106

ISBN: 9781625493705

Poetry Editor: Kevin Walzer
Business Editor: Lori Jareo

Visit us on the web at www.wordtechweb.com

I am so very grateful to all you Nimrod Hall writers who shaped this collection, especially Charlotte Morgan, artist-in-residence.

Contents

I

II

III

I

Jefferson Hospital Emergency Room, 1959

A nurse under a stiff white hat looks at the gash on the back of my head, takes me to the metal sink, washes my scalp and shaves off a little bit of hair.

This, she tells me, is a sterile field.

She puts me on a table, under a double-sided blue-green sheet with matched binding around a hole in the middle.

If I do not move, I'll go home sooner.

The hospital is an old house we pass on the way to church.

The intern sewing up my head
is learning from Dr. Trout, who got up from supper and walked over when dad brought me here.

A man and woman bang on the front door, straight down the hall from where I am lying. They shriek and beg for treatment for their child but no one lets them inside.

In the car, on our way home, I ask dad why I got treated but those other people were turned away.

He flinches and does not answer for five blocks.

Through clenched teeth, he whispers they were sent to *their* hospital on *their* side of town.

In that moment, my father's reaction to the other family's care becomes more important to me than the split in my skull.

Molly Lee

I sit on the gray hooked rug. My back leans
on the couch where I'm sometimes allowed
to sit and watch TV with my family. I practice

my name while everyone else is at school.
I write Molly Lee over and over, working hard
to keep the o, body of y and e between

dotted and solid lines. I know
my name has to fit in a certain space.
After lunch, mom promises to take me downtown

on the bus. I love climbing up steep rubber steps,
the hiss when the door closes and looking at all
the faces of people I don't know. When they pull

the cord to tell the driver where to stop
I wonder where they live, what work they do.
"Curiosity killed the cat", mom says.

Molly Lee. I practice on paper without lines.
I think I have it. The only other requirement
for me to worry about is if I'm tall enough

to stand at the counter and print my name.
If I do both today, I'll check out my own books
at the Roanoke Public Library.

2212 Broadway

We shared one bathroom upstairs
at the end of the long hardwood hallway,
across from the sleeping porch.
No lock on the door.

My sister's first teenage fight
with dad was her pleading
for a lock on the bathroom door.

This spacious room featured
a claw foot tub on the right,
sink and mirror straight ahead,
commode next to that with an overhead
window, four panes on a frame
that opened with a metal latch.

Three people functioned in there
at once doing different things.

I watched my father shave in front
of the mirror. All of us did.

He left the door open in case
of necessity. Mom plopped my brother
in the tub with me, left us to wash
with sponges and a waterwheel.
We yelled when we wanted out.

I never remember a bath uninterrupted.
Somebody always needed the sink or pot
or mom had to open the window or take
a bottle from the blue medicine cabinet
my sister refinished.

My older brother got dibs
on the toilet after school
before he left for ball practice.
If the door was closed, I knew to wait.

I never questioned that then and I don't
question it now. Waiting my turn.

Winter Memory

Cinnamon cold the morning
cloudless blue the sky
sugar dusts the platter
sleders wait outside.
Finely ground our memory wakes
to a whiff or textured taste.
Cinnamon cold the morning
cerulean blue the sky.

Clyde Cooksey

That spring Alan Shepard became the first American launched into space. Grandma and Grandpa Lee were so excited about it, their enthusiasm spilled over into our household. All four of us kids were playing astronauts on the covered side porch of our house when mom called us into lunch. Tommy put Gordy in his highchair and the rest of us took our places at the kitchen table to eat peanut butter and jelly sandwiches with Fritos and milk.

"Mom, how come Grandpa knows about all this space stuff?"

"Grandpa's an engineer, Tommy."

"Where are our other grandparents?" I asked Mom.

"You only have one set of living grandparents, Molly. You know how my mother died. My father's dead. I've told you this before."

"What was his name? I forget."

"Margaret, finish your milk," she replied.

She called me Margaret when I'd done something wrong or when she wanted me to know the conversation was over.

After lunch we all had to rest for an hour which meant we could nap or look at books or read. No talking allowed. That day, Tommy and Gordy went up to their room, Shannon and I looked at books downstairs and Mom took a nap in her room with the door closed, just like always.

I was on the maroon velvet couch in the front parlor with Shannon when the doorbell rang. I hid behind the parlor door when Shannon walked out into our large entry foyer to open the front door. A nice-looking man in a sport jacket asked Shannon if Mary Pennock was at home. That got my attention because most people call my mother Penny.

I thought Shannon was very polite when she said, "And who shall I say is calling?"

He took off his hat and replied, "Clyde Cooksey, her father."

Shannon left the front door ajar, turned and looked at me with her mouth stretched in an exaggerated "O" sign and her eyes wide with surprise before she ran upstairs to tell mom. I just stood there. He couldn't see me but I could glimpse him standing there in his coat and tie, through the window panel beside the doorway.

I don't remember Shannon coming down with her but Mom came downstairs and opened the front door all the way. She barely paused to look at him before saying, "Don't you ever come back here again." She slammed the door in his face and went back upstairs.

I don't think mom ever knew I was there.

After School, 1967

Our screen door always hits a heel of my shoe when I come through the front door.

"Mary, how come the Butler boys always get away with being mean? Henry put a daddy long legs down my back on the bus and the driver didn't even threaten to call his mom."

"Mrs. Butler will get a call and she'll punish him, alright. She just has too many boys and she can't keep up with all their carrying on when their daddy's away. They'll settle down. Just try to ignore whatever Henry does unless it's nice."

Because mom and I are both five feet tall, we borrow each other's clothes, especially skirts, slips, and sweaters. These are the items that work for both our ages. Our borrowing custom is to check to make sure the other person isn't planning to wear a certain item that day, like culottes or the pale yellow McMullan blouse, and if the borrowed item can't, for some reason, be returned to the drawer or closet where it belongs, it's ok to store it where you'd keep it if it was yours. And whoever needs it next is free to go fetch it back.

As a seventh grader, I understand our shared use agreement is not common so I don't tell anyone when I wear mom's clothes.

This morning, I put on my new blue checked skirt that mom made me for my birthday. I turned thirteen yesterday.

"Molly, I can see light shining through that skirt," Mom says when I come down for breakfast. Mom has drilled into my head that if I wear a skirt or dress the sun shines through, a slip is required so I go find the half-slip from her underwear drawer and put it on.

After I talk with Mary, since I know mom's napping, I go to my room to change my clothes and put the borrowed slip in my underwear drawer. When I pull the handles and open the drawer there's a highball glass laying on its side in the front of the drawer and there's a little tomato juice in the bottom of the glass. The juice has been there a while so it's congealed to the glass. And it smells like it's mixed with medicine. I'm so surprised, I just put the glass back where I found it, stuff the slip over it and close the drawer. I pull on my hip-huggers and go down the street to see my friend.

Before supper, I check and the glass is still in my drawer. I bring it down to the kitchen to show mom.

"Do you know why I found this glass in my underwear drawer when I got home from school?" I ask.

"That's the most ridiculous thing I've ever heard of," says mom, and she acts like she doesn't know what I'm talking about. I just stand there, my arm stretched toward her with the glass in my hand. When she sees I'm not backing off she says, "you're being impudent. Go to your room and don't come out until you are ready to apologize."

When my father arrives from work, he comes up to check on me in my green room. I'm on one of my twin beds, listening to the radio. "Can't you just apologize to your mother for being disrespectful and come on down for supper?" he asks.

I dig in my heels. "There's no reason to apologize. I just want to know why a dirty glass was in my underwear drawer."

Dad doesn't give me a reason and he doesn't let me off the hook. I spend the evening in my room with no supper.

Smoothing the Creases

I ride the bus from school.
Mary rides the bus to work.
We'll drive her home when dad
gets home from work. I plop down
on linens she's sprinkled,
piled in a side chair.
I eat my Hydrox. She tells me not to
spill on the whites. Moles barely show
against her polished skin smoothing
creases with her thick hands. We talk
about anything that comes to mind—
her children, mama, Henry Butler's
latest prank and whether Jesus
really had blonde hair and blue eyes.

Family Squall

There you have it—
one of us utters
a sentence so sharp
it pierces
and drains us
lifeless,
walking along
this wide sandy beach
as a family
after breakfast,
imposing solitude on each of us,
while the whimbrel
scuttles ahead
pecking foam
on the ocean's edge
then tracks its prey
to stab and suck,
leaving only shells.

Stamped and Sealed

Dr. Sandra Briel, one of my biology professors, stops me in the hall to ask if I have time to meet with her and Dr. David Briel, her husband, also one of my biology professors.

I walk upstairs with her to their shared office. We all sit.

Sandra says, "we have something for you."

David hands me an envelope, stamped and sealed.

The return address is my trusted mentor and cell biology lab supervisor. The letter's addressed to the Medical College of Virginia Admissions Office.

I am the only student at Longwood applying to medical school.

David suggests I read it to decide if I want this recommendation to go forward. If not, he and Sandra will provide another.

The letter of recommendation is a tawdry account of an academic misfit with too-numerous-to-count sexual innuendos.

Over the past few years, the Briels tell me, they have witnessed the careers of other students ruined by similar letters written by the same professor.

This morning, when they saw this letter in the Biology Department out-box, they decided to snatch it.

Getting Even

I don't remember my aunt with us, outside, watermelon juice dripping down our play clothes. Twelve cousins spat seeds at one another. Grandpa and our parents had fun telling stories and spat too. Grandma always plopped an oval zinc bowl in our midst. We ate watermelon so she could pickle the rind.

When the container was full, I followed grandma inside and helped scrub and peel the skin, trim teeth marks from the green-white flesh. We put the rinds in her bathtub to soak overnight. I always had to go home before we finished.

At Thanksgiving we all crunched her dark green treat in sweet and spicy syrup.

During college, my aunt showed up in her Italian shoes to take me home for grandma's funeral. My funny uncle, Whimpy, drove us. As soon as we got to my parent's house, she marched into our dining room, and in front of all my family, barked at my father to give her grandma's wedding rings. Her tone was sour and I knew it hurt his feelings. Dad was grandma's youngest and lived in the same town so he took great care of her and her possessions. When my aunt visited, I saw her take things from Grandma's: a linen tablecloth, cloisonné vase, a skillet.

Several years after Grandma died, I was at my aunt's house. I found the watermelon pickle recipe.

Now it's mine.

Friday Night Jamboree

Down the road past Schoolhouse Fabrics,
Cockram's Store faces State Route 8,
just west of Main. By day, bare wood wears
smooth with shoppers hunting overalls,
work boots, and gloves. At 6:30 Friday nights
after a supper with pippins and kraut,
string players appear and merchandise
gets pushed aside. Benches from the porch
move inside, a fiddle tunes, claw hammers
chase the melody. Outside town
forks of the Little River run down
both sides of the continental divide
and native trout spawn. By dark, licks
and picks and tunes and spoons clap
from the alley and parking lot. Kids move
from set to set. Inside, cloggers clop
to the featured band, name posted in pencil
on a paper taped to the wall since last
week. Out on the porch, guitars swap
picks and upstairs banjos roll a fetching
tune as the worn wood floor pulses
inside Cockram's store. No matter
who attends tradition stands:
Obey Granny's Rules or leave the site
No smoking, no drinking, no spitting or cussing
from 6:30 until 11:00 on Friday night.

Meeting Jim Crow

Between the four hospitals at the Medical College of Virginia in 1978, there was a network of almost-lit tunnels underground. Other students told me Confederate soldiers dug these tunnels during the Civil War. Supposedly, they were started as escape routes before the city was occupied. This labyrinth led to and from the hospitals and was less crowded than the hospital hallways and, as a medical student, I learned these tunnels almost always provided the quicker route to transport a patient wherever they needed to go for tests or treatments. As I recall, there were only two actual destinations located under the hospital, obtainable through these subterranean passageways: Cobalt and the morgue. One good thing about these underground corridors was how they spared patients from getting snow and rain on their sheets and gowns as they were sped from place to place. The downside was the dim light and those tunnels always smelled like a dirt cellar in March with last season's onions rotting with mold and sprouts.

As a third-year medical student, I was expected to do any and everything a patient needed. The interns, residents and attending physicians assumed their students would make sure patients' tests were completed and posted in the chart, x-rays read, and transportation secured. When it came to transporting a patient off the floor, I just did it myself.

On the afternoon my first patient coded, I had taken her to Cobalt. I wheeled her there from North Hospital, with help from her husband. He visited her days and played trumpet nights. While we rolled her, he reported news of the Grammy winners and told her about the new Harriet Tubman stamp. I saw him tap his thumb on the bed rail and pat her hand to the beat of a tune he hummed to her. Once we got

17

⌐ Cobalt, he waited outside the door, marked with a huge magenta radiation trefoil. I left him in a steel gray space without chairs, while I took her into the treatment room.

The radiology technicians worked from a radiation safe-station between two treatment rooms; one for whites and one for blacks. My patient was in the latter and shortly after I joined her husband on the outside of the treatment room, a siren groaned to the beat of a sign flashing "*Treatment In Progress.*" During the middle of her treatment, someone yelled for help so I crossed into Cobalt.

My patient was splayed for radiation, jagged mastectomy incision burned and raw from gamma rays. Her face slurred, still warm. Through her dark skin, even I could see gray replacing pink. I had no idea life could escape so fast. We tried resuscitation. The others' efforts at chest compressions seemed uncommitted. I blew harder. When the attending pronounced her dead, everyone scattered like roaches when lights turn on. I had to ask for help, twice, to move her back onto the gurney, techs already busy in the white-patient room. I smoothed her hair and tried to shape her mouth relaxed. I considered how I'd want to hear what I had to say to her husband, still out there waiting. I knew, too, I'd have to ask him to help me roll her back through the tunnels, from Cobalt to the morgue.

Ferning

1. a forage into the under story,
   gleaning species adaptable
   for transplantation,
2. a clinical term used to describe
   the pattern of secretions harvested
   on a slide to determine pregnancy,
3. a Saturday in the woods
   examining spores and cuts and stems
   to know a sensitive fern from a lady

Grade, Psychiatry Rotation

"Your answers are inadequate."

"But you said there were no right or wrong answers."

He smashes the butt of his cigarette into the onyx ash tray, looks up and blows his last drag into my face.

I turn my head to avoid the nasty yellow smoke.

He says nothing. I decide to wait.

"You obviously don't agree with my interpretation of the human psyche," he says.

"Freud's," I say, "is not the only way."

"What do you prefer?"

"I prefer to assess a patient and decide if there is psychosis, neurosis, or any pathology at all.

Most humans aren't psychotic and can be analyzed for preferences, neurosis, or psycho-social idiosyncrasies."

"Even women?"

"Yes sir."

"You fail. This conversation is over."

Sawmill

While she does the dishes, he finishes
the barn chores, slips through the stile,

cranks the engine and slides green oak
toward the saw blade to slice like butter.

She hangs clothes on the line he strung
between maple and walnut posts.

When she smells fresh cut locust
she knows the blade will hum dull,

drops the wet wash in her basket
and walks through the pasture

stippled with tickseed. She motions him
to follow. He catches her hand

under the willow. By the river
his leathered hands lift her to the ground.

Sounds of water over rocks drown the sawmill
motor left running in the sun-drenched hollow.

Euthanasia

Once a friendly foal, now sick and old.
Nothing to do but by the bridle hold
with grain in hand and gun and dread
you walk around the cliff to meet the cold.

Back to the house you trudge in deepest dark
with empty bridle, bucket, gun and lowly heart.
To walk to death accompanied by a friend
must surpass the final walk apart.

Once Weekly, As Directed

First, leave the asphalt
to traverse spaces
where ferns and their allies
can't not grow,
cross mountain streams
to score your mind
with the music
of burbling water
over rock
so that lists, facts
and details
shrink to fit dimensions
they deserve.

Then rest someplace
where heat from sunlight
or wood fire
penetrates each and every sinew
to completely relax
your anatomical core.

Broke Scrub

My community medicine assignment, as a fourth-year medical student in 1980, was to go to Nassawadox, a remote town on Virginia's Eastern Shore, and do a community surgery rotation. I anticipated it with positive expectations. I knew I was a better than average surgeon and, in a small community hospital, I'd be the only person in the operating room with the surgeon and staff. I'd get lots of different opportunities to perform surgical techniques and do plenty of suturing. It was there I planned to decide if I really wanted to become a surgeon.

I shared a suite with my friend, Jamie, and one of his buddies. The food was fabulous. Fresh oysters were served at least once a day. It was January, a proper 'R' month for Chesapeake Bay oysters.

My surgery supervisor was Dr. Boyd. He was well trained and seemed to love rural life. We scrubbed together for a few days and things were going about as I expected. One great thing was how warmly the nurses welcomed me, a female surgeon, and how delighted they were to have a teachable medical student, eager to learn everything they knew.

On the first Thursday of a four-week rotation, I thought Dr. Boyd stroked my left breast with his gloved hand during the operation. This didn't really make sense to me as it would mean he broke scrub and contaminated his hands during surgery. Since that was unthinkable to me, I dismissed the incident as a faulty perception on my part. But the same thing happened on Friday. He definitely broke scrub. On Monday, Dr. Boyd set a time for us to have a coffee conference where he informed me I'd be having lunch with him at his home from now on. I fumbled an excuse about another operating room commitment to avoid it that day, but he insisted every day. Each demanding request revealed a bit more detail about his expectation which involved his bed, while his wife was at work, and my grade.

At this point I talked to Jamie about Dr. Boyd's behavior. He did not disbelieve me but he had no idea how to respond to my situation. During our conversation I decided I'd spend all day every day assisting whichever surgeon was in the operating room. There was no problem arranging this with the nurses so I had a fairly good experience doing surgery with the other surgeons and, when scheduled, Dr. Boyd, who was now downright hostile towards me. I simply kept every interaction with him on a student to teacher plane and asked lots of surgical questions.

The rotation ended. I returned to MCV. About two weeks later I was summonsed to the office of the chairman of my faculty advisory group, a cadre of men who kept an eye on me academically and would conduct my oral exam later that semester. The whole group was there when I arrived. The chairman, a thoracic surgeon, asked me "what the hell happened over there?" I was taken aback and asked "why" suspecting what was about to unfold. "You're one of the best surgeons in our fourth-year class and Dr. Boyd gave you an 'F' for your community surgery rotation. Can you help us understand what happened over there?" For some reason, against my better judgment, I told them the entire truth.

There was silence. I was dismissed.

Two days later I was summonsed back to the advisory group chairman's office where they were all reassembled. The thoracic surgeon asked "is there any other surgeon over there you spent enough time with to ask for a second evaluation?" I was floored. Those good ole guys believed me! They were sympathetic and were giving me a way out.

The second evaluation demonstrated an above average student. During my oral exam, a few months later, despite the tales of terror from my colleagues about their oral exams, these men asked me the easiest possible questions and conducted the process in a spirit of fellowship and collegiality. They told me I'd learned what I needed to know.

II

Transmogrification

It happens when I float in a tube down
the middle of a river lined with oaks,
sycamores and banks of bluets early
in the season, or jewelweed and black-
eyed Susan later on. I float along
and what I used to call dragonflies
dart every which way: Eastern blue
darners, violet dancers, biddies and common
skimmers. One lands on my leg. It doesn't
matter what state or which river I'm
floating; what I now know to call a damselfly lights down on my thigh. The damselfly
holds her wings above the body, her flight
tentative. Because I know she'll appear,
I've looked up and learned about
these insects to find some meaning
in this tradition, or maybe it's a ritual;
me and damselfly floating the river
together. I know this is her last instar,
the stage she's expected to reproduce.

She probably hatched this same time
last year and crawled through fall and winter
from weed to stone clinging to rootlets
when lotic waters grew too strong in spring.
About the time it was warm enough for me to shed
my gloves and start to fish, she climbed
up on some rock for her last appearance.

The last time I floated, the scenario
changed. An American Rubyspot hit
my leg just past the low water bridge
on the Cowpasture. She mated some guy
right there, but that's not new. She stayed
on my leg for four miles, till I landed
at the dock, then flew off and hovered
while I loaded my tube in the back seat.
Then she landed on the hood and her hind
wing caught between the chrome strip
and the paint. She flapped and flipped
to free herself, her spiracles fluttering
open and closed till we both rested.
My mother always told me I'd mess up
the balance if I touched a small flying thing
so, I didn't. Like a diva composing herself
for a performance, she posed on the hood
and slipped that hind wing from under the chrome
strip and vanished. Seconds later
two rubies shimmered above the river,
tethered to a ray of afternoon light.

Glenna

tore her hand on the ring washer.
Earl determined she'd see a doctor.

Newspaper told of this new lady doctor
in town. Glenna said she'd go there.

Her wound, ripped like old wet tissue,
needed an expert. Glenna wouldn't have it,

said I could do as good as any city
doctor. She watched me fumble

the first stitch, then unraveled
her life story while I sewed edges

that never matched. When we were both
satisfied, she made a plan for me to check

her wound on my lunch break, said she'd
rather fix me dinner than have some agency

inside her house. During daily dressings
at her kitchen table, we watched Earl

come in from the fields and climb
the back steps for dinner. When I left,

after dessert, the porch swing rocked them
shelling peas or snapping beans.

Flaws and Frays

I can't throw away seashells. Or hand-me-down
linens— perfect for an heirloom quilt I say—
snips of lace sewn in the curve of a bodice
worn on a wedding day, Irish napkin corners,

hollowed in the center, piles of cutwork
patterned from slender threads, pulled one
at a time. A single snip in tatted trim
unravels weeks of work like family stories

rend carefully bound flaws. Why not expose
them like edges of velvet? Comb the fray,
sculpt the lint into soft and supple padding
for flowers in ribbon, silk, cotton and flax.

I stitch these pieces and bits together
intent to mend and reuse beauty
from cloth so ruined with rips and stains,
there's barely space for weft to hold warp.

His Chief Complaint is Headache

Slumped in the straight back chair,
in the corner of a room in need of paint,
his dark eyes meet mine as I enter.
He does not return my smile.

The interpreter introduces us. I explain why he,
an Afghanistan refugee, is here to be examined.
We review his medical history.
He admits to indigestion and impotence.

His chief complaint is headache.
I examine him. Scars on his square head.
His affect, depressed.
I sit. He and the interpreter continue.

For eighteen months he slept on slate,
was starved and tortured by the Taliban.
They put his head in a vise or beat it or
kicked it. He rarely slept for eighteen months.

We talk longer than the schedule allows.
He says it is good for the U.S. to be in his
country. He hopes to go home someday.
I hug him before he leaves.

Some months later I see him with his
family, waiting to pick up medicine
from the pharmacy.
Today he smiles back.

Sallying

I enjoy the privilege of traveling
undisturbed, a dusty road, throat

bone dry, waiting for a peek
at tanagers, redstarts, and pheasants.

A purple martin's tail pokes
from a nest cheeping with babies.

A host of flycatchers forage
by the Missouri. Clustered

in a tree branch, they wait
for prey, then fly out and sally

over waving grass to seize dragonflies
that breed this morning. Each bird

returns to eat and wait. Cottonwood
fluff lines roadside ditches.

Ferns are thigh high. A red-tailed hawk
gets pecked all the way to kingbird's boundary.

My grandchildren will pay handsomely
for such delight. They'll purchase a chance

for a shift in a viewing blind and pay
extra for Coke or a glass of champagne.

Pre-Op Bathroom

Corners caked with enough dust to sprinkle
graves of every patient admitted
to pre-op this morning. Baseboard's one long
continuous scar. Shredded panic cord hangs
on the wall where scuffs and dents record
collisions with wheelchair
handles or poles hanging un-
pronounceable fluids. Socks snag
dirt off the floor beneath the toilet.
My patient asks if the O.R.'s clean.

March

"a magical time when the river and the season and the bird all come into brief conjunction." Paul Johnsgard

This is the season I get anxious
for geraniums to bud in their pots
on the laundry room window sill

but the sun is weak as a young crane
who must fly between a pair of adults
at the end of a long day. The bugle cry

in their bones is ancient as their footprints
on shallow wetlands where sunset
reminds them to lower their legs against

the wind and land for the night.
By day, these cranes gorge to double
their weight on last year's corn

left in fields beside the river,
where they dance and toss sticks
before leaping through snowmelt

to navigate bitter wind over frozen prairie
begging for the sound of meadowlark,
sprigs of Indian grass and big blue stem.

Geranos is the Greek word for crane
and the root for geranium. Each year
before sun turns hot enough to dry

my clothes, the whistle call of Sandhill
cranes pierce the heart of the sky
where the Platte converges with the season.

At the Wise County Fairgrounds

I sit in a rusted metal chair
taking a history from my patient,
half dressed, behind old cotton sheets
cinched with hemostats to simulate
corners of an exam room. I startle
at a flare of camera flashes that,
for an instant, properly illuminate
cinderblock walls of an exhibition barn
turned medical clinic, whitewash-splattered
dirt stuck to my feet. We blink.
I apologize for the disruption, our unlit cranny,
stale air and ask if she's comfortable
disrobing for the breast exam,
hold up a frayed hospital gown
for a second shield as she removes her bra.
She tells me the men and women with press
passes roam the grandstands recruiting patients
to shadow through the maze of exam stalls,
lab, pharmacy and the dental chairs located
under blue and white awnings. She doesn't
mind the carnival, cameras or the heat.
She's waited all year to stand in line
for this chance to see me at the fairgrounds.

The Rose in My Front Hall

I steal a tea rose from Memorial Park,
tell myself I'm pruning.
I pluck the bloom above
the third fifth leaf
and walk over thousands of petals
fallen to the ground.

My husband scorns me for stealing
but I persist. I love even the thorns.
The fragrance lingers like a balm
as it smooths my limbic sulci[1],
nursing wounds from all the pricks.

---

[1]The limbic brain system involves motivation, emotion, learning and memory; sulci are grooves
in the brain.

Pollinator

You hover over native waterleaf,
slender stamens and violet petals
sway in your direction.

I watch you work one plant after the other,
your long tongue extracting nectar
honeybees can't reach.

You move to the next wildflower
waving above the forest floor
woven of maidenhair ferns. Bumble

buzz softens as you tune vibrations
to shake pollen from the flower.
Reminds me of my lover trembling

above me. The flowers appear
unscathed. As I head up Sprout's Run
nettles sting my legs.

Tall Grass Prairie

I walk early to spot birds I've never seen.
Hazelnuts and apple trees trim the edge

of the prairie. An unfamiliar siren
draws a red-tailed hawk from a sycamore

and steals morning silence. Neck hairs stand.
Unstirred air brushes my skin.

The temptress pauses for my thoughts to settle
then wails again, warning me and the dickcissel

perched above an unmown meadow fluttering
with red-winged blackbirds. I stiffen,

distracted by the sound, and walk on.
Beyond the giant cottonwood, the path turns

down by a pond. My mood softens for a mother
and her fawns, unperturbed by the incessant

whine that prickles my skin.
I walk fast by the trail marker

past the bend. Across the road a rusted
windmill twists the wind, round and round.

She charms water to the surface screeching,
When prairie disappears, dickcissels follow.

Stonewalled

To the beat of your lifelong drum
the height of your wall extends,

stone on hard cold stone. By the time
I get home from work, you've slit

sweetness from daybreak's kiss,
blocked your hold around my waist,

skin to skin, dogs nuzzling for warmth.
This stonewalling sours the moment

our tongues taste succulent morels you've
prepared for us with brandy and cream,

locks you in darkness when evening light
invites us to wander under redbud's last

bloom. I see life recede through holes
in your wall. I whisper *I love you.*

Crack filler splashes (and stings) my eye
from the safety of your side of the wall.

Supermarket

Over the aisle of canned tomatoes
comes the rankle of discontent
between mother and child,
continues past baked goods
and produce. Beside the paper plates
a smack resounds.
In the silence that follows,
I load my cart with the shame of every child
and the pain of every parent.
When wailing blocks the frozen foods.
I go to check out with my basket full.

Touch-me-nots

It's mid-July and jewelweed banks the road.
In summer, green grows languid in the woods
with orange and yellow blossoms all aglow.

One summer hike he carried the heavy load
when nettles stung his legs and drew his blood
in mid-July when jewelweed banked the road.

She dipped jewel leaves in water 'til they shone
then rubbed them on his skin right where they stood
with orange and yellow blossoms all aglow.

Smitten by a natural cure bestowed
he bid her lie with him, then said they should
between the tallest jewelweed and the road.

For many summers a single track they wove
through fern lined thickets spiced with cedarwood
and orange and yellow blossoms all aglow.

Since he's gone, she walks this path alone.
Touch-me-nots court memories with their pods
hung on verdant shrubs beside the road
with orange and yellow blossoms all aglow.

Hunting Morels with My Son

You suggest I leave work early, head for the base
of cottonwoods, oak, elm. You say they're best
in batter, fried like green tomatoes. I defend

morel gravy I made last year. We used to comb
the beach when you were small. You filled
your fists with shark's teeth.

Today you want to cover a lot of ground,
tell me south facing slopes are best and bolt.
I crawl on my hands and knees. The lining

of cracked hickory shells glisten in
sunlight, unfiltered through leafless trees.
Every other catkin tricks me into thinking

it's a morel. We're three inches behind on rain,
the soil's still cool and a dozen bird songs fill
the air. You reappear with a deer rack, five

points intact. In the pleasure of your company
I overlook you're jobless, do-less, lost.
We note the only wildflower in bloom is violet,

white and purple gloves hanging from tart stalks.
Garlic mustard's ready to flush, leaves zing
our tongues. You say you like a reason to leave the path,

tromp through the woods seeing trees from another
point of view. It's important work, gathering wildness.

In Omaha

On the fourth of July
you can join a parade
led by your postman
followed by dressed up dogs,
your neighbors,
a spate of strollers glitzed
in political paraphernalia,
five Democrats,
and Susie Buffett's dog
to sniff your crotch.

David Miller's Trail

(U.S.F.S. Ranger David Miller disappeared while hiking alone in
Secret Mountain Wilderness, Arizona, 1997)

Canyon wind whips my bones. Aspen leaves
rot on ground where weak sun forces a final
bloom from aster and short stem lupine.
You're still not back. I wonder what your

last night was like, play it back in my mind
again. Water in your pack, fresh drawn
from the creek, you intend to find a way to link
sides of Secret Canyon. I start out with you, hike

where morning scents of pinion pine and cypress
vie with juniper and heath. You say we're born
to walk, evolved erect to take it
at our own pace; once accustomed to the geography

beneath us, the footing changes. You tell me
geology forms the face of the ground we walk on:
red rock, lava crush and run, limestone sand.
A herd of javalina bristle when we approach

Dry Creek. The trail ended there so I sent
you on your way, alone. Now, a stretch of trail
is built from there to honor your scheme
for a circuit hike through your favorite canyon.

This morning, golden moss lights rock and youthful
prickly pears shine upside the canyon. I wonder
if your end came from a predator raking your throat
or a desert thirst. Pain is such a lonely place.

While a raven circles round and round again
as if he sees your remains, I spot globes
of pale berries hanging from high branches.
It's time to gather mistletoe.

Your Promise

"I will not leave you comfortless:
I will come to you."
John 14:18

I think I see you leap
from flying buttresses, turn
out for autumn, and appear
sliver-mooned through
The Needle's Eye
in Custer, South Dakota.

I work hard to find
you with me cooking
rice or in the completion
of a well-ironed pocket.

I hope you're present
in the whisper of a patient
and the pain of knowing
that, however hard my day,
a neighbor will ask for help.

Your promise dangles
like larvae
floating in lazy water
encased,
never to leave home

until the caddis fly breaks
water, carrying itself
from sunken cover to catch the wind.

I see you there with silky
threads on translucent wings.

Eastered

I see why it feels like home, sitting
in this hard pew at a strange church
on Easter Sunday, feet propped
on the kneeling bench. It could be the sea
of navy-blue blazers over oxford cloth collars
cinched tight with knotted bows
or the waft of perfume from ladies
wrapped in extravagant fabric
or the hats—floppy brims with ruched
flowers, straw ones and veiled caps,
one trimmed with a grosgrain
fan that waves at me.

It could be how the altar stands
flush against the reredos, widening
the gap between God in man and me
or how easy it is for me to regress
to catty thoughts of how this congregation
can afford three associates,
a theologian in residence,
plus the priest.

I remind myself to be nice:
it's Easter, the first Sunday after the first
full moon of the Spring Equinox.
Two nights ago, I watched the moon rise
above the Peaks of Otter and ate
fried green tomatoes with my sisters.
Yesterday, a flight delay delivered

me into the arms of an old friend.
We combed the woods behind her house
to find Spring Beauties plunged
in sunshine, the right condition
to loosen winter's fierce embrace.

Even though the tips of redbuds barely show,
the sun is warm outside after church in a garden
of chilled air stirring camellias, daffodils
and a genuine smile from my daughter.

Whiskey and Blood

She's talking to the officer while I glove up

Somebody called the cops when I lost control,
They took my kids to safety.
He got real mad when I told him
he didn't need any more to drink.

I smell whiskey as I press and release
her wound to examine the depth
of the jagged tear down the bleeding
arm of this mother of two under two.

So he whacked the whiskey
bottle on the counter and came at me
with the broken edge.

I numb the gash and start stitching.

My period's late too, she says to me.
He's in jail
I'll live with Granny for awhile.

From a chair in the corner,
Granny hums Roy Acuff tunes as I mend
her granddaughter's wound.

I don't need to drink anymore; but he
can't stop: I just want my babies back.

After some time, I count sixty-six
stitches.

Grandma sings out loud

Who did you say it was brother?
Who was it who fell by the way?
When whiskey and blood run together
Did you hear anyone pray?

Electronic Medical Record Training

tab click options app
password not your name
inbox open template task
providers are to blame

start with nursing master doc
toggle quick or real
HPI assess and plan
code to close the deal

phone encounter drug advice
labs from out of town
build the record document
but patients slow you down

orders schedule P.A.Q.
office note review
no more writing no more books
see patients P.D.Q.

secret sexual history screen
needs its own alert
else the information gleaned
is buried in the dirt

bring your virtual patient up
don't ignore the tasks
forget about the human face
flesh will never last

but Dragon and e records
make everlasting tomes
don't forget to logout
before you leave for home

Kitchen Table

More than where I start my day,
it was once a tree,
walnut home for birds,
nut factory, and shade.

Just the spot to write a novel
about characters who sat around it,
playing poker aboard the Mississippi gambling
boat for which it was designed
complete with crafted hatches for storing guns,
napkins, books, crayons, binoculars,
bandages, journals, cards.

It's a place where neighborhood
children bring their friends for cookies
or an open wound in need of a bandage,
where tea is served to a Lost Boy
who doesn't want butter on his toast,
or the table where the Bishop of Bradford
takes black coffee with his biscuit

My children ask me questions here, the ones
they've been holding back or tell me
which drugs were used at the party last night.

This table holds a peripheral brain
of shopping lists, menus, and reminders.
It's a solid slab of necessity
where all my worlds converge.

Prairie Grace

Close to a prayer

Grant me strength to stir the squall within me
to glimpse entrusted realms beneath my feet
where flame fires dirt, scents brew the air
and supple grasses bow as you draw near.
Plant inside me seeds worth sowing,
refreshed with after-burn for growing.

Thanks to Elizabeth Bishop

I'll tie up my walking shoes,
put on that shark's tooth and coral necklace,

grind coffee beans and enjoy the smell.
I'll read "The Filling Station" to engage my core.

I might read it again, sip my coffee
and watch hummingbirds outside.

Just listen to those crows.
They're up there scheming whose corn to steal.

Because mama always talked about whether people
lived on this or that side of the tracks,

I walk with my head held high enough
to see above the tracks

and watch for sticks and stones along the way.
I let dirt get under my fingernails,

pick unripe tomatoes, am careful what I say.
I don't play bridge. Sometimes I stumble

when I walk and with no sense of direction
I start from a new spot every day.

Good Morning

Strawberries
will never be fresher
or sweeter.
Scarlet curves
cannot fatten more.
The flesh drips
with juice.
Go ahead,
bite the berry
and make this moment
burst open
your day.

Autumn Wedding

The *plein air* painter dabs color on canvas
propped beneath a sycamore that sags
from the bank of the Jackson. I cast
my fly into a colorless pool shimmering
between his dappled hues.
We intend to catch what isn't ours
but want the best of each to find.
When I ask the painter
why the light's so clean,
he says dry air and the slant of the sun.
Daylight draws shade from the stream.
We see a pair of dragonflies take
hold of one another, mid-flight
like the couple who'll wed on the riverbank
this afternoon when the fish quit biting.
We're invited here to see his nut-brown hands,
her rosy lips, their kiss.

Jackson River

Crotch deep in snowmelt,
with plans to hook
that trout I missed last time,
he hits my fly.

I strip, stop at twelve o'clock and two
as I've been taught,
then startle at a dark force
under my line.

A paddle tail breaks water
smashing its greeting
in the silent stream.
I am honored, beaver.

Red Cow

The farmer finds a newborn calf,
delivered of a small red heifer
in a patch of wild onions,
both of them cold,
lying in new grass.
He watches the calf stand
untrained. It wobbles away
bleating for nourishment
and warmth to survive.

The new mother rouses,
wanders off looking for her calf
she cannot recognize
apart from the place of birth.

He sends his son to a neighbor's
dairy barn for colostrum.

For five days,
drudgery upends the farmhouse.
Each member feeds the calf
from a bottle.
Un-nuzzled, un-licked.
Abandoned, thin.
Likely to die.

Interruption at the Hovelow*

Unexpected thunder. No chance
of rain. Sky rumbles the rolled
tin roof. Outside, a blackcap
chickadee shares sunflower seeds
with purple and gold finch
till lightning splits
the northwest sky.
Silver tips of autumn olive
rock and wave when birds
take cover. The dog barks
at a welcome breeze.
A biker spins gravel the sound of current
frying wire. I sit down and rock
and wait for rain. Another streak rips
over Caldwell mountain.
A stiff wind stirs the smell
of burnt beets left boiling on the stove.

* **hov-e-low** (huv'a lo'), *n.* **1.** substantial structure of significant age,
shaped like a bungalow, with numerous defects of a hovel

Sunset

Moments after
fireflies rise
to twilight,
a low lying
Morse code
of innuendo
commences.
I see two flash
together,
then land naturally
as goldfinch pair
on a hackberry bough.
Burden of midsummer
heat dissipates.
Mountain air blackens.
Coupling's complete.

Great Blue Heron

Your in-flight squawk wakes me,
predawn, beside the Corotoman.

I don't know what sight provokes
your voice or whether you intend

for me to stir. Over the bank,
I watch you land, stilted legs

anchor in black mud, rich as truffle
butter. From water's edge, your gaze

guides mine. Grey trunks of loblolly
pines trace light where we sit in wait.

Each moment clears a shadow and draws
the current of my shallow life deeper

until urgent cries from crows and gulls
drag me back to the surface.

Headed for Work

Along Virginia Route 11, dogwoods
verge to bloom. Flashing lights
of an oncoming car warn
me to take it slow around
the next curve. Three cows
lumber across the highway.
Out-fenced. Unaware. Full.
At some point in the morning,
the farmer will notice them
gone. He'll catapult
into retrieving two blacks
and a brown. By noon,
the cows will graze
with the herd
inside a mended fence,
and the farmer will not
have accomplished one thing
he had planned for the morning.

Drawing the Cork

When I step off the path,
fog-wrapped aromas baste me

in pulverized limestone, waxy
galax, rusted rattlesnake

ferns and sassafras.
Huckleberries, beechnut crumbs,

eggshells and dogwood blight
funnel through night crawler

casings, pine cones,
deer drop and maple sap.

Bouquets complex as fine wine
steep from mash under foot—

leaves packed on squaw root,
sarsaparilla and walnut decay.

Occasional beams of sun bake shale.
Where greenbrier pricks the sky,

blue suffuses the mixture,
finishes with richness of place.

After the Last Gully Washer

Five hours ago, you and my brother raked
gravel back into the curve of your driveway,

flushed to bedrock during the last
gully washer. Then you said you

didn't feel well, like a vessel
was about to pop in your brain,

and you keeled. He did CPR,
called 911. Your neighbor helped.

Now your temperature's ninety-four.
Warming blankets blush your skin,

earlobes and lips. A girlish haircut
frames your unlined face.

He strokes your hand, so devoted, work
gloves still stuck in his back pocket.

I lift your smooth eyelids.
Pupils fixed and dilated, unresponsive.

His mind knows you're gone
but his heart can't let you go.

The nurses trimmed and cleaned your nails
for this last date with your husband

where he holds you in some afterlife
between brain death and whatever's next.

Fall

I know it's fall
when slanted shafts
of late season light
unveil rock ledges,
snails and pebbles
beneath purple mistflower
or the heat of the sun
warms my toes
in counterbalance
to the cool of the shade
on my shoulders
relaxed, in the hammock
strung between walnut and oak.
Days are perceptibly shorter.
The dog whines early
to trot down the street
and play with children
waiting for the school bus.
These are favored days.
Lettuce is up,
lime green in brown rows.
Peppers pickled in jars,
windows wide open
all day and all night.
My skin shrinks.
Wrinkles wick lotion
before going to bed.
Quiet accompanies
the change in light.

This is the time of year
I allow myself to know
I've already lived
more days than remain
to hear the church bell
clang. I pull into myself
and decide whether to risk
dabbling with color
in plein air light
or resent the inevitable darkness.

An Aging Druid Princess

wears her long hair down, and fun smart shoes,
forages for food, hunts mushrooms 'til noon,

shares her wealth unconventionally, looks out for the poor,
cooks kindly for the frail and loves sex at sixty-four.

She swims naked at night and plays under the moon,
takes the infirmities of age like a square dance tune,

shares her secrets of life with the young and the old
while she continually learns to grow her own soul.

Tribute

Dear Will and Clay,

This is what I wanted to say at your mom's memorial service.

My name is Molly Lee; your mother was my first friend.

In 1957, she sat next to me at my third birthday party where she wore a green smocked dress with a white collar and bow tied at the back of her waist, with patent leather shoes and dress ankle socks.

She lived up the alley from me, and up the street, but the alley was quicker and more interesting.

Her oldest sister and my older sister were good friends.

We also grew up in the same church and our parents were friends.

At some point we were allowed to walk to each other's houses, BY OURSELVES! That alley became our road to many life lessons.

There was a vacant lot across the alley from my house which was the epicenter of daytime neighborhood activity.

Her backyard was the epicenter of nighttime activity, most notably, kick-the-can.

We did what we wanted as long as it didn't catch the watchful eye of her other sister.

ear older than me so we each had other friends and
different schools.

I spent the night with her on Christmas night for many years (and
as the middle child of five, that was something to look forward to
after the chaos of Christmas at my house).

At her house, there were always cases of soft drinks (SunDrop was
my favorite), mixers and Charles Chips stored in the basement.

My first notion of a planned healthy snack was in her refrigerator,
where there were always cut up carrots and celery with a slice of
onion soaking in water inside a covered glass container (of which I
now have two).

Her parent's cocktail hour was most tolerable because they allowed
us to hang out and play cards or something on the side porch while
they drank and talked or we were allowed to watch TV from the
cushy couch in the den until supper was ready, after they finished
their cocktails.

The reasons I liked to play with your mom all those years ago turned
out to be traits she evinced throughout her life:

> She loved to laugh (and she had the same twinkle in her eye
> as her dad)
>
> Her idea of having fun involved being outside
>
> She didn't mind getting dirt under her fingernails
>
> She was curious but not reckless; in fact, it was from her I
> first saw the benefits of considering the possible
> consequences of an action before taking it (like building our

first fire in the alley) or consider the various ways one could pull off a project before diving in (like constructing a ladder from the trash cans behind our garage to the roof of the garage where we could spy on everyone)

She did not talk about others behind their backs

I could trust her completely

She didn't prattle; conversations and play with her was always meaningful

With your mom, three girls could have fun— no one gal out triangle stuff

She enjoyed my company and respected my point of view

In high school, of course, she became completely involved with your dad. He adored her and she him.

I smoked my first pot with your mom, during high school, sitting on a blanket in the grass on the side of the road along the Blue Ridge Parkway where she drove a bunch of us in one of the family's old Cadillacs.

My friendship with your mom established the foundation for which I aspire to be "a friend".

When I opened up my solo practice of medicine in Botetourt County, in 1983, your dad's aunt and uncle became patients of mine. His aunt was also a teacher and a farmer. Good people. They loved your mom. Through them I was able to keep up with the milestones in your lives, like your births.

I missed our active friendship all those years she was raising ya'll in Powhatan, teaching, as I was raising my children and working.

I am so grateful we reconnected in 2014.

We had some great walks, heartfelt conversations and texts, new book ideas for one another and much affirmation of a life well lived.

May stories, pictures and memories with your mom enrich every day of your lives.

Fondly

Molly O'Dell

Environmental Health Specialist Senior Retires

Sun glistens from leaves of the magnolia
tree he must have planted to shade the yard.

From the bottom of the driveway his wife stops
herself from saying the chest he aims to carry

is too heavy. His wasted frame lifts
his blue wood crate, scuffed and scratched,

filled with its familiar contents—
rock hammer, survey flags, metal clipbox,

drain field cheat sheet and hornet spray.
He shuffles toward the trunk of my car

with this tool box, employing every muscle
left in his upper body.

It's love that directs her silence.
She and I could transfer these objects

ourselves. But discharging his auger, animal
head cooler, unused calendar and tools

back to the agency provides him closure
for thirty-seven years and his life's work.

Frozen

I proceed past Solitude, unincorporated.
Jennings Creek carves ice and snow
tumbling towards the James.
Just after dawn, the trail head sparkles
with melt from a solstice moon.
Dirt surfaces on weeks of old snow
banked beside the path.
My feet crunch oak leaf plaster,
pitted red and black on white.
I follow the wind's whisper
up switchbacks to Bryant Ridge.
Hemlocks thrive among scrub pine,
defy predictions on their demise.
I breathe in cedar.
There's no need to rush thaw.

For Barry

Look for a lady slipper to discover trillium.
Search for a kestrel to see cattails change

from corn dogs to cotton candy
over the course of a single season.

Watch for waterfowl and see how beaver
work their way through cottonwood.

Spy on junco to enjoy the shimmer
of milkweed fluff snagged in small

branches this sunny winter day. Hunt
bald eagles to get spotted by an owl.

Wander after snow geese to find a new
path of wildcat prints frozen in the snow.

My patient, Barry, taught me always to look
for something; it's discovery that keeps us well.

Great Valley Overlook

Common milkweed greens flap beneath silver
pods, goldenrod blooms and stickweed.

Daylight thins over distant ridges,
still warm enough to wait without a wrap.

Your presence approaches like a swarm.
The stun and thrum of it

gently settles in my chest when you sit
down beside me, at the edge of the meadow.

I toast you, awkwardly. With moonshine.
And we talk. We finally remove our dark

glasses. Your brown eyes meet my blues.
Twilight trims our silhouettes with sparks

so natural, I let you slip inside my fence,
leaving the gate wide open after the sun sets.

Notes

"Winter Memory" is a response to Eric Fitzpatrick's watercolors *Winter Memories; Stanley Avenue Sledding and Thoughts of Coming Home*

"Euthanasia" is for Chuck Conner

"Autumn Wedding" is for Dover and Betty England

"Aging Druid Princess" describes Katie Letcher Lyle

"Tribute" celebrates my friendship with Claiborne Gooch Hammond

"Environmental Health Specialist Retires" is for Mike Campbell

"For Barry" is for Barry Kinsey

Acknowledgments

I am indebted to James Broschart, Linda Thornton, and Elizabeth Colen for their critical input on this manuscript, Kathy Dudding for her editing expertise, Susanna Byrd for creating the cover art for this book and Adam Johnson for my photograph.

Thanks are due to the editors of the following periodicals and anthologies in which some version of these poems and prose first appeared:

Adrift: *Headed for Work*
Artemis: *Touch-me-nots*
Calyx, A Journal of Art and Literature by Women: *Broke Scrub*
Celebrate: A Collection of Writings By and About Women: *Kitchen Table*
Chest: *EMR Training* and *After the Last Gully Washer*
Derondo Review: *Stonewalled*
Family Medicine: *Meeting Jim Crow*
Feeding and Fasting: Reflections for the Lenten Season: *Smoothing the Creases, Hunting Morels with My Son, Your Promise, Eastered,* and *Interruption at the Hovelow*
Hospital Drive: *Autumn Wedding*
Kaleidoscope: *David Miller's Trail*
Main Street Rag Anthology Show Us Your Papers: *Molly Lee*
Medical Encounter: *At the Wise County Fairgrounds*

Medical Literary Messenger and Amendment: *Jefferson Hospital ER, 1959*
Off the Chart, WordTech Editions: *Glenna*
Pine Mountain Sand and Gravel: *Flaws and Frays*
Plainsongs: *Prairie Grace*
Platte Valley Review: *Sallying*
Poetry Leaves: *Once Weekly as Directed*
Traveling Poets Society: *Sawmill*
Untidy Season: *Pollinator* and *Transmogrification*
Virginia Literary Journal: *Jackson River* and *Great Blue Heron*